Scottish Landscapes

Photographs by
Colin Baxter

Text by
Jim Crumley

LOMOND BOOKS
EDINBURGH · SCOTLAND

Scottish Landscapes

Scotland is a rocky place. Its profile is tousled by islands, mountains and cliffs. Even its green lowlands are beset by dark volcanic hiccups, gaunt rock souvenirs to jolt a sense of place just when it might have been in danger of becoming becalmed.

But what a repertoire of rocks! What a geological ragbag, from Jurassic upstarts a mere 150 million years young to ancient Lewissian survivors 3,000 million years old. From the sea-worn masterpieces such as Dore Holm in Shetland to St Kilda's ocean-going cluster of island-sized sculptures; from the bony ridges of the Skye Cuillin to the unforgettable monolith of Suilven; from the high and vast-skied plateau lands of the Cairngorms, with their overtones of the Arctic, to the Gulf Stream dowsed Ailsa Craig; from the crumpled and understated might of the Border hills to the gannet-white Bass Rock, footnote to the Firth of Forth which would not look out of place in St Kilda. The show never ends.

And what beautifully lit rocks! Scotland may not have the most consistent climate, but the very changeability of the light is a crucial factor in the landscape's charms. Generations of artists have sought out that light and its quick-fire moods, which seem to change the very hues of

THE CAIRNGORMS
The mountain massif of the north-east Highlands with scattered Scots Pines, outliers of the distant Abernethy Forest.

BRODICK BAY,
Isle of Arran (opposite), in the Firth of Clyde.

LOCH BRACADALE,
Isle of Skye, with the
islands of Oronsay (left)
and Wiay.

the rocks themselves. The trick is particularly potent among islands, where the infiltration of seas compounds the sorcery, but no part of Scotland is immune to it.

The other landscape element you remember is water, not just for the blatant way it tears and wearies away thousands of mainland and island miles of coast, but for the way it softens even the starkest of rockscapes and makes arenas out of mountains. Loch Coruisk, in the Cuillin, is a celebrity among waters which Turner elevated into something phenomenal and other-worldly, with only a modicum of exaggeration and a perfectly logical skip of the imagination. It is that kind of place. Set his canvases alongside those of Joan Eardley, whose uncompromising seascapes have turned Catterline on the north-east coast into a kind of artist's Mecca.

Then there are waters which become the whole landscape, and the surrounding shores and hills merely artefacts to hold the thing in check. When you add the immense depths and a healthy monster legend to 22 miles of lochside, it is easy to fathom the lure of Loch Ness.

Salmon rivers (Tay, Spey, Tweed are among the chieftains of that clan), moor-freckling lochans, bellowing waterfalls with knee-trembling names

like Glomach and Grey Mare's Tail, goose-loud firths and otter-quiet sea lochs...these are the great waterscapes of Scotland, each in its own way as compelling as an ocean storm smashing lumps out of a Shetland headland.

So it rains in Scotland. When you weigh the benefits of water in the landscape to sunshine after storm (November in Wester Ross is the place and the season for connoisseurs of rainbows!) and the crucial role of jealously guarded spring water in the alchemy of single malt whisky, you will forgive the weather almost anything.

There are softer, greener shades to the Scottish landscape too. The Ayrshire of Robert Burns; the Carse of Stirling where the coiled river snake of the upper Forth meanders far below the hills and woods of the Trossachs and the great rampart of the Southern Highlands; the rich farmland kingdoms of the east coast - East Lothian, Fife, Angus, Buchan, the soft whisky hills of the north-east; Orkney, where low slung islands flatten under skies the size of oceans.

The landscape has fuelled more writers than Burns (although arguably none better). Scott made the Borders his own and shared Edinburgh with Robert Louis Stevenson and Norman MacCaig (whose poetry lingers as

ARD BAN
Classic west coast,
near Applecross,
Wester Ross.

GREY SEAL PUP

LOCH DRUIDIBEG,
South Uist.
A National Nature
Reserve noted for its
extensive machair.

WILD IRISES
Common throughout the
Western Highlands and
Islands.

fondly in Sutherland as in Edinburgh); Angus and the Mearns produced J. M. Barrie and Lewis Grassic Gibbon; Neill Gunn's was the voice of Caithness and East Sutherland, and George Mackay Brown's poetry, short stories, novels and essays relate the life-blood of Orkney. The West Highland landscape was the heart of much of Gavin Maxwell's writing, and Seton Gordon was a restless luminary of the Highlands and Islands. Skye is Sorley MacLean's, and all Scotland gloried and winced in turn under the explosive scrutiny of Hugh MacDiarmid, and at his best, he was maybe the best since Burns.

The very destiny of Scotland, the nation, has been shaped (and misshaped) by the landscape. It is no accident that men chose to make

capitals in turn out of Stirling and Edinburgh, where singular rocks – stubborn volcanic plugs in a chain stretching from Dumbarton to the Bass Rock – were converted to all but impregnable fortresses.

Robert the Bruce chose to fight under the symbolic strength of Stirling one summer's day in 1314, and because he had the time and the strategist's mind, yoked the landscape to his purpose. His enemy Edward I and his army made the disastrous error of

TRÀIGH SCARISTA & SOUND OF TARANSAY, HARRIS

THE WEST COAST OF SOUTH UIST

LOCH AFFRIC,
West Highlands, with
early snow on the
mountains clustered
around the head of
Glen Affric.

camping in a bend of the Forth, and with the since immortalised Bannock Burn on one flank, found themselves pinned by the impenetrable shiltrons of Scots spears. Crucially, this situation cramped Edward's cavalry, the hammerhead of his army, and denied the possibility of their ferocious charge. Bruce and the landscape won the most memorable battle in Scottish history.

Charles Edward Stuart, Bonnie Prince Charlie, could have done with Bruce and his awareness of landscape at Culloden Moor in 1746, when the retreating and ragged Jacobite army finally turned to face the pursuing Duke of Cumberland on a gaunt moor near Inverness. The Prince, who had been dissuaded by his chieftains when he might have marched on London itself, now overruled them and insisted on defending what was an

indefensible position. You get no sense of the slaughter which occurred on the Bannockburn battlefield today, but you can still walk far out onto the moor of Culloden, look around you and shake your head at what was done there.

BEINN ALLIGIN, Torridon. Seen from across Loch Torridon, Wester Ross.

But of all the landscapes of Scotland, it is to the mountains that most visitors to Scotland are drawn. They hold a special place in the hearts of the natives too. Their landscape is what others judge us by. And whether we think of ourselves as Highlander or Lowlander or Islander or something else, we all look to the mountains as the backbone of our nation. We are shaped by them. They give us our stoicism, our reputation for hospitable shelter, our temperament of storms. The mountains are Nature's enlightenment. They are her greatest works.

But to see the mountains for what they are, we should first step back, back beyond their reach, to the fringes of the realm. Shetland was mountains once. Their worn-down summits are the islands of northernmost Scotland, although in truth there is more here which owes its allegiance to the Norsemen than to the Scots. At Lerwick you are nearer to Oslo than Edinburgh and London is a thousand miles away.

URQUHART CASTLE The castle against a moonlit Loch Ness.

The landscape is different too, sliced up by long voes and sounds, and named by Norse tongues, Yell, Whalsay, Burra, Papa Stour, Foula, Trondra, Quiarff. And Muckle Flugga,

of course, that northernmost stutter of
what is collectively called 'Britain',
though a less British place you would
be hard-pressed to imagine. It is like all
the island extremities of Scotland, a
place of spectacle.

It would be convenient to uphold
Muckle Flugga and Hermaness as the
great showpiece among Shetland
landscapes, but the first name on that
roll call is surely Westerwick. The red
granite of Westerwick is not so much
red as pink, making a fantastic horseshoe of cliffs with the ocean in the
bottom, as glorious a definition of that
Shetland word 'wick' (the Norse *vík*, a
bight) as you could wish for. As bights
go, Westerwick's cliffs are tiled with
the ocean's teethmarks, its sea surface
littered with the crunched fragments of
the land. It is not beautiful so much as
mighty. At the slackest of tides on the
calmest of days it is not peace which
reigns but impatient tension, eager for
resumed hostilities.

*PASS OF
KILLIECRANKIE,
Perthshire, in the green
glow of a new spring.*

The same war of elemental attrition – the ocean against the rock – is
the prevailing state of St Kilda, forty miles west of the Western Isles. St
Kilda redefines the word 'island' as here the landscape's every impact is
vertical; islands with thousand-foot cliffs and stacs which leap 600 feet
out of the ocean and glower blackly down while boats creep tinily by.

There is a third combatant in St Kilda; birds in such numbers that they
rival the landscape in their impact...the biggest gannetry in Britain. There
are puffins in uncontemplatable numbers (but come and see what
300,000 pairs look like, and wonder how anyone came to a conclusion on
their numbers), fulmars that get under your feet and fly past your nose,
bonxies (great skuas) that draw a bead on your head and are not shy of
hitting it. And in the midst of all that cacophony there dwells St Kilda's
own sub-species of wren, a sweet-voiced survivor with a taste for airy
singing perches.

*LOCH AWE,
Argyll
(opposite), coloured
by the seductive shades
of dusk.*

LIATHACH
The mountain master-
piece of Torridon,
towering over Loch Clair,
Wester Ross.

Seasonal wardens and a reluctant Army contingent live here now, since the islanders were evacuated in 1930. A visit there now is not a wholly edifying one, but there is no landscape like it in the country, and few in the world.

On one of the rare clear days (a handful in a year) you might climb to the summit of Conachair on St Kilda's main island of Hirta and see, far, far to the east, a blue blur of island shapes. Your binoculars will perhaps pick out the white scratches of beaches – Harris perhaps, or Benbecula, or the Uists. Mostly, Conachair reveals no land in any direction through 360 degrees, and you gain your first shuddering insight into what it took to *live* here. Far beyond even those distances, you might catch a glimpse of an impossibly distant saw-tooth skyline – the Cuillin of Skye, first stronghold of the mountains.

Harris is a hunched place, and you suspect it was born looking ancient. Like much of the Western Isles, it is certainly ancient now. This uncompromising terrain is composed of 3,000 million-year-old Lewissian gneiss, the oldest rocks in Britain, and among the very oldest in the world. From any vantage point at all (the two most recommended are the

summit of Clisham, more than 2,000 feet above the Atlantic, or a window
seat courtesy of Loganair), the wonder of the place is that it supports
human life at all. Then, when you find the human life, you notice that
much of it is ranged along the western seaboard despite the unprotected
view of prevailing Atlantic storms, despite the absence of natural
harbours. But when you notice that the east coast is bald rock and dark,
but the west wears a ribbon of green between the white beaches and the
rock, the reasoning becomes clear. The machair is the sea's gift, sweet
grass on a shelf of shell sand. Over many years man has fertilised it with
seaweed, chemicals and the dung of grazing beasts. In
summer it blossoms brilliantly, with carpets of tough
flowers, a fragile toehold of fertility grafted onto the
rock and peat mass of the islands, a straw for crofting
families to clutch.

These west-facing beaches all along the Atlantic
seaboard of the Long Island (collective name for the
Western Isles from Lewis to Barra and its acolytes) are
among the most delectable and untrampled shores
anywhere, even if their climate is rarely fit for
sunbathing. That evening sound which sets your teeth
on edge, as if someone was dragging a comb across a
matchbox, is the bird emblem of these islands, for
they are almost the last stronghold of corncrakes. Few
birds have suffered quite so catastrophically from
changed agricultural practice as the corncrake. Now
the grasses and iris beds of the Uists, Lewis, and Coll
are their last sanctuaries.

LOCH BROOM,
Wester Ross.
A solitary lobster boat
heads home for Ullapool.

POST BOX,
Red Point, Wester Ross.

NEIST POINT,
Isle of Skye.
The lighthouse looks
out over the Minch
to the Western Isles.

Skye always beckons, whether you approach from across the Minch, across Kyle Akin, the Sound of Sleat, or nose head-first into the matchless gabbro of the Cuillin by way of Loch Scavaig on a northbound yacht out of Rum, there is no dull landfall on Skye. Gabbro is wondrous stuff to climb, imparting an almost magnetic adhesion to a human skin, but it is sharp-edged too and takes a fearful toll of boots and breeks and fingers. But when it is heaped up into the Cuillin's relentless horseshoe of skinny ridges and pinnacles and prows it is unforgettable. It scarcely matters whether you dance among the summits or dawdle through Gleann Sligachan looking up, or drive over Glen Brittle's monumental steeps and hairpins – proximity to the Cuillin is never anything less than an adventure-in-landscape.

Indeed, all Skye is just such an adventure, a remarkable repository of landscape contrasts. The Sleat peninsula in the south (pronounced 'Slate', not the fatal 'Sleet'!) is low hills, countless lochans and fragments of old woodlands (although its claim to be the Garden of Skye is pushing it a bit – for trees in a Hebridean setting, try Mull and relish the difference!). Cheek by the Cuillin's jowl are the Red Cuillin, sleek, steep hills,

spectacular if strenuous walking hills, and the best viewpoints anywhere
for contemplating the Cuillin.

The heart of Skye is moorland. And the west layers basalt lavas up into
a matching pair of plateau-topped hills, MacLeod's Tables, a landscape
centrepiece for the hereditary MacLeod chieftains to admire from their
stronghold of Dunvegan Castle.

Then, when you think you have seen all that Skye can throw at you,
you stumble on the geological showpiece of Trotternish, where the weird
rocks of the Storr and the Quiraing have dropped the jaws of travellers for
centuries. What has happened here is that another basalt lava plateau has
been tormented from beneath by the retreating ice when the last ice age
finally caved in. Thus weakened, the mass collapsed into landslides
leaving such bizarre rocks as the Old Man of Storr, the Needle, the Prison
and the Table for us to gawp at.

Enough. It is time to put this island lingering behind us and step ashore
at Kyle of Lochalsh. We have tested the mountain realm in the rarefied
isolation of the Cuillin. It is time to immerse in that sea of mountains,
the Scottish Highlands, but Skye is not left entirely behind.

SHIELDAIG VILLAGE
On the shore of Loch
Shieldaig, the village lies
sheltered beneath the
Torridon mountains.

15

THE RIVER SPEY,
Boat of Garten.
One of the Scottish rivers
famed for salmon, and in
recent years, for ospreys.

EILEAN DONAN
CASTLE, Loch Duich.

There are four great demarcation lines among the landscapes of mainland Scotland – three faults and one thrust. They are the Southern Uplands Fault, the Highland Boundary Fault, the Great Glen and the Moine Thrust. This last named feature heaved old rock westward on top of young along a 100-mile tumult from south-west Skye to the north coast of Sutherland. On Skye, the effect is not particularly marked, but as you journey north through the north-west Highlands, the mountains become more and more sensational. You may think you have seen it all by the time you have confronted Torridon where Beinn Alligin, Liathach Beinn Dearg, Beinn Eighe and Slioch jostle outrageously. Here too, the bedrock Lewissian gneiss, onto which inconceivable masses of Torridonian sandstone were heaped, then whittled and pared away to what today are – incredibly – mere stumps of what has gone before.

That Moine Thrust laced the mix with other delights, notably that glittering, banded white quartzite which graces Torridonian summits, and Durness limestone betrayed by pockets of emerald fertility amid the great rock wilderness. Suilven encapsulates the whole thing, arguably the most mesmerising mountain in the land, the

ultimate marriage of the Lewissian and the Torridonian, and from its heights you see, in the midst of so much rock and water, the miracle of Elphin's greenery to the east, and you know from that small stain that Elphin is a limestone fluke.

Rivers here are short and fast. Trees are rare, the more welcome when they do occur in numbers. Loch Maree is swathed in blue-green Scots pines, a remnant of the great Caledonian pine forest, and the islands in the loch, un-felled and ungrazed, show how thick on the ground the trees once were. To many people, the very bareness of the Highland landscape is part of the attraction, but in many places it is an imposed bareness, induced by centuries of felling and more recently the browsing of too many red deer.

Trees have provided many controversies in the Highlands, and far to the east of the Moine Thrust and straddling the borders of Sutherland and Caithness lies a vast area of blanket bog as much water as land – the Flow Country. Biologically, the place is priceless, one of the most important of its type in Europe. At its heart is the national nature reserve of Blar nam Faolieag, but here, in the 1980s especially, the subsidised craze for

LOCH GARRY
A famous viewpoint on
the road between
Invergarry and
Kyle of Lochalsh.

planting conifers has wreaked havoc. At risk is both the habitat itself and its fragile flora, and the breeding grounds of moorland birds, notably greenshank and dunlin. Not all Highland places are high or even land.

And when you stand in the midst of the flat farmlands of Caithness and remember again the great individualist mountains of the west on their miles-wide plinths of ancient rock, it is difficult to grasp that, as the eagle flies, you have travelled not much more than 60 or 70 miles. All you have done is make a typical traverse of the country from west to east, a pattern which is repeated almost anywhere in Scotland.

A line of Sorley MacLean's poem, *Kinloch Ainort*, reads, 'a great garth of growing mountains', 'garth' being an enclosed garden. So, it is a great garth of growing mountains which masses ahead of you as you head south towards the Great Glen, that great glacial slash which cuts diagonally down the face of the Highland heartland from Inverness to Mull. The Great Glen holds Loch Ness, among others, and the Caledonian Canal, and in the midst of all that mountainous might, boasts a watershed only 115 feet above sea-level.

It is a watershed among landscapes, too, and south and east of it the

18

power of the mountain mass intensifies for reasons not easy to name. It may be something to do with the increasingly land locked nature of things, and certainly by the time you have crossed the Great Glen as far as Creag Meagaidh above Loch Laggan, stockpiles of mountains reel off in every direction and there is no hint of either ocean or sea.

ACHNAHAIRD BAY and the landscapes of Coigach, Wester Ross.

Creag Meagaidh is a good place to pause, as here, a miracle of nature has been worked, nothing less. The mountain was bought by the Nature Conservancy Council in 1984 when its flanks were about to be smothered in cash-crop conifers, and its faltering mountain birchwood was doomed. The NCC's purpose was restoration of the whole mountain fauna from lochside to summit plateau. The means was to kill huge numbers of deer.

SOAY, ST KILDA (opposite), and (below) a resident puffin.

It was a long-term exercise and continues under Scottish Natural Heritage. Parts of the mountain which once held a thousand deer now hold 200.

The birchwood's restoration is astonishing, far exceeding the wildest dreams of the project's founders. Orchids and many other mountain flowers now flourish. The mountain is restored to health, and provides an object lesson about the true nature of the beauties of Highland landscapes for all to see.

BORDER HILLS, Characteristically blunt-shaped and green.

CUL MOR AND STAC POLLAIDH, Inverpolly National Nature Reserve, Wester Ross.

Even Glencoe was wooded and fertile once. And lived-in. Although much has changed there, so much has not. In particular, it remains, of all Scotland's landscapes, the most potent progenitor of myth and misconception, a landscape in wolf's clothing; who hasn't looked at the place on a grey-black day of curtaining rains and pronounced it the vilest place on earth? And with a hundred inches of rain a year it offers no shortage of opportunities for you to curse it.

'The Glen of Weeping' is now a fanciful and discredited translation of the name Glencoe, but research has only taught what the name does not mean and scholars still search for a definition. For all that, the landscape still weeps, and rain imparts a curious tension about this glen's close-gathered walls. There is too, the old salt-eyed stain of the Massacre of the Macdonald clan in 1692, which it seems must forever darken the name Campbell. For all the atrocities in the repertoire of man's inhumanities to man long forgotten before and since, the Massacre of Glencoe still offends – not just Macdonalds, but millions of neutrals the world over. Facts merely confuse. It was just one more outrage in an era which thrived on outrage. As a massacre it was a desperate botch – 38 died and 300 escaped. Many still contend, its notoriety lingers because the principle of Highland hospitality was abused. Or perhaps it is the very nature of the Glencoe landscape, both intimidating and introverting, acting as a brooding preservative, a conducive arena for the conjuring of old bloodsheds.

But there is another Glencoe. On the Rannoch Wall of Buachaille Etive Mòr and many a gully and ridge is the trail of Scotland's mountaineering history. All its great names have trod this stage and graduated to the most famous mountains in the world. At its toughest, Glencoe ranks with the severest tests mountaineering has to offer.

BROUGHTON PLACE
This handsome building, nestling in the Borders near Peebles, is built in the style of a traditional borders tower-house.

THE NORTHERN CORRIES OF THE CAIRNGORMS,
from the air, showing their dramatic glacial scoops.

From the summit ridges of Glencoe's crown, Bidean nam Bian, the Highlands sprawl away in every direction; yet even on that singular summit, and among all the other mountains, one massive shape overwhelms. From any distance, and from any direction there is no mistaking the one we call simply 'The Ben'.

Uniquely among Scottish mountains, Ben Nevis is undiminished by distance. Even the vast scope of the Cairngorms looks almost benign from afar. The Ben, so often horn-locked with its own storm, so contemptuous of human life at every level of mountaineering competence, has never learned to affect meekness. From 50 miles or 50 yards, it is the monarch of all it surveys, commanding immensely. Its impact on both the landscape and the minds of men has spawned a long and distinguished literature which shows no more signs of abating than the flow of mountaineers and hill walkers. Thousands who never climbed another hill and never will, stumble up as much of the pony track – 'the yak route' – to the summit as they can endure. To stand on the summit of Scotland is Everest enough, for on a clear day the summit of Ben Nevis is the most astonishing place in the land.

Down then, and south to where the mountains yield at last and offer up a gentler country. The Scottish Lowlands begin with the Highland Boundary Fault, another of those fundamental demarcation lines which runs south-

MOUNTAIN HARE,
in its winter coat.

west to north-east from the Clyde, right through the islands of Loch
Lomond, leaving its indelible imprint clear across the country to
Stonehaven on the east coast.

Small towns (where a certain quintessential Highland Edge Scottishness
dwells, neither Highland nor Lowland but moulded by both) stand at the
portals – Callander, Crieff, Dunkeld, Kirriemuir, poised places, calmly
rooted on that most fundamental of all Scotland's landscape divisions. To
the south and east, the land grows more and more fertile, the climate
more benign – or at least less eventful.

Short ranges of lesser hills rise up out of the fields – the Campsies, the
Gargunnock Hills, the Ochils, the Sidlaws, hillwalking terrain of subtler
shapes and shades and immense vistas. The Gargunnock Hills west of
Stirling give the clearest imaginable illustration of the geological
principles implied by the Highland Boundary fault, by straddling a vast
swathe of it before your eyes. Ben Cleuch, summit of the Ochils has
sightlines from Ben Nevis to the heart of the Borders.

Shallow lochs and reservoirs lie in the shadows of these hills, sanctuaries
for vast numbers of wildfowl. The Lake of Menteith and Loch Leven, for

*THE MOUNTAINS
OF KINTAIL AND
GLEN SHIEL,*
*from the high tops on a
clear winter's day.*

OLDSHOREMORE,
near Kinlochbervie,
lies on the north-west
coast of Sutherland,
which is renowned for
its unspoiled beaches.

example, lie at the heart of tranquil landscapes of great wildlife riches. The Loch of the Lowes near Dunkeld has become a new landmark in the confident southward expansion of the osprey out from its old stronghold at Loch Garten on Speyside. The bird's wavering hunting silhouette is now a familiar sight on many a loch and river, but the public hides at the Loch of the Lowes and Loch Garten offer unique bird-watching opportunities, and bird-watching takes on a whole new dimension of wild theatre when ospreys are involved. If you thought gannets were good fishermen, your first osprey is likely to make you think again, and the bird is now much more than a Highland recluse.

The nature of the Lowland landscape is coloured by three great firths or estuaries – the Clyde in the west, the Tay and the Forth in the east – each

serving the needs of three of Scotland's four main cities – the Clyde's Glasgow, the Tay's Dundee, the Forth's Edinburgh. Aberdeen is out on its own lowland limb far in the north-east, built on the river Dee, and dispensing with the need for a firth by perching on the coast of the North Sea.

LOCH NA KEAL
Haunt of golden eagles and otters, on the west coast of the Isle of Mull.

The rocks which underlie the fields of the Central Lowlands are comparative newcomers by geology's standards, belonging to the Carboniferous age which places them at about 300 million years old. A fruitful pot-pourri of rocks they have proved too, not just because of the agriculture they have sustained, but also for exploitable riches - coal, shale oil, limestone, ironstone, sandstone and clay. One way or another, the Lowlands have provided Scotland and Scots well. Two-thirds of the population live there now, and although historically and culturally the Lowland Scot differs and has a different language from his Highland and Island compatriots, he moves easily between realms and if he thinks of his country from afar he thinks not of a land of cities and fields but of a country of mountains. Few places in Scotland lie beyond the force-field of the Highlands, except perhaps that southernmost realm which has its own hills, crammed in the self-containment of the Borders.

IONA ABBEY,
Isle of Iona.

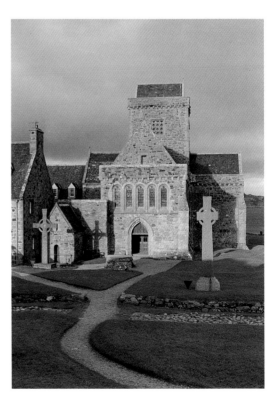

If you would look for a linchpin between Lowlands and Borders, you might find what you are looking for in Edinburgh, a city with a distinctive landscape of its own. It has its own small mountain at its heart in

THE BASS ROCK,
Firth of Forth.
A gannet citadel of the
East Lothian coast.

Arthur's Seat, and nature was the principal architect of its Old Town, built on the volcanic castle rock. As the capital city it exerts its sphere of influence in every direction, even reaching across the Forth in the mighty spans of two great bridges. But somehow it feels as if, essentially, it is bound to the Borders by the thread of the Pentland Hills.

So the last of the four great demarcation lines of Scotland has been crossed – the Southern Uplands fault. In doing so, you have been ambushed, almost without realising it, by blunt hills which close at your back and throng the land clear to the English border. Eastwards the landscape of the Tweed evolves and softens towards Berwick; westwards lies Ayrshire and Galloway, where gannets and golden eagles and red deer remind you of where you have been. But if there is a reservoir for the traditional stoicism and independence of spirit which has long been associated with Borderers, it lies in the hill country occupying the old counties of Roxburgh, Selkirk and Peebles.

History's imprint is indelible on this landscape; the hills and valleys embrace and hold a sense of the past in much the same way as Glencoe enshrines its Massacre. The great bulk of the Devil's Beeftub is as

uncertain a place on a dark day. But to toil up out of its depths, on and on up to the summit of Ettrick Pen is to step from a hell of a kind into a bright-skied heaven.

You usually toil to traverse your Border Hills, but once you are up, you can walk at around 2,000 feet for miles amid the exhilaration of golden plovers and mountain hares, then dive down some dark gully to find a four-square peel tower at the foot, a dark brown and seductive river, such as the Yarrow to accompany you through an intimate valley, and a hostelry where you least expected one.

It is a dull soul who cannot respond to such a day by delving into the ways of the Reivers – Borderers who free booted among the hills not out of military duty or devotion to a cause, but as a means of making a living during the turbulent centuries of strife between Scotland and England. From this distance, they cut romantic figures, although the reality of their

lives, which depended on looting from their neighbours to make ends meet, was as laced with hardship and tragedy as it was spiced with adventure. Like so many aspects of the Borders, their like did not exist anywhere else in Scotland.

So it is with the Border Ballads, a unique peasant tradition of verse-making, which captured the imagination of the young Walter Scott. He grew up on his grandfather's farm at Sandyknowe through the 1770s and

THE SHETLAND
ISLES
Becalmed and storm-
bound. Ronas Voe (above),
Eshaness (opposite) and
Thrift (below).

1780s. Nearby Smailholm Tower, one of the most enigmatic of peel towers (souvenirs of that long era when every Borders community needed a fortress to withdraw into from time to time), must also have fired Scott's imagination. It is not possible to overstate the worth of his collection of 1799, *The Minstrelsy of the Scottish Borders*, for it ensured an audience for the ballads and determined that in time Scott himself would unfurl the Borders' most distinguished literature, one in which the inimitable landscape was its bedrock.

Scott cast his writer's eye all across Scotland, but it was to the house he built at Abbotsford and all its surrounding miles of Border lands that his heart was thirled. He made a single view of the Eildon Hills famous simply because he loved to stop and stare at it. It is said that when his funeral cortege passed the spot his horse stopped there unbidden because it had grown so accustomed to doing just that.

Every year now, thousands of visitors come to pause above the same bend in the Tweed. They see the heathery trinity of the Eildons shapely above wooded fields. For many of them it will be the beginning, that day when unwittingly they allowed the landscape of Scotland to creep in under their skin.

ST NINIAN'S ISLE, and its tombolo sand bar, Shetland.

GLEN CLUNIE, near Braemar, Deeside.